First World War
and Army of Occupation
War Diary
France, Belgium and Germany

39 DIVISION
117 Infantry Brigade
Sherwood Foresters
(Nottinghamshire and Derbyshire Regiment)
9th Battalion
1 March 1916 - 30 September 1918

WO95/2587/6

The Naval & Military Press Ltd
www.nmarchive.com
Published in association with The National Archives

Published by

The Naval & Military Press Ltd

Unit 10 Ridgewood Industrial Park,

Uckfield, East Sussex,

TN22 5QE England

Tel: +44 (0) 1825 749494

www.naval-military-press.com

www.nmarchive.com

This diary has been reprinted in facsimile from the original. Any imperfections are inevitably reproduced and the quality may fall short of modern type and cartographic standards.

© **Crown Copyright**
Images reproduced by permission of The National Archives, London, England, 2015.

Contents

Document type	Place/Title	Date From	Date To
Heading	WO95/2587/6		
War Diary	Mazingarbe	01/02/1918	01/02/1918
War Diary	Hulluch-Left Sub-Sector	02/02/1918	08/02/1918
War Diary	Mazingarbe	09/02/1918	13/02/1918
War Diary	Hulluch Right Sub Sector	14/02/1918	21/02/1918
War Diary	Mazingarbe	22/02/1918	25/02/1918
War Diary	Left Sub Sector	26/02/1918	28/02/1918
Heading	33rd Infantry Brigade 9th Service Bn. The Sherwood Foresters War Diary March 1918		
War Diary	Trenches Hulluch Sector North	01/03/1916	05/03/1916
War Diary	Mazingarbe	06/03/1916	10/03/1916
War Diary	Hulluch Sector South	11/03/1916	16/03/1916
War Diary	Hulluch Sector Support	17/03/1916	26/03/1916
War Diary	Line Locality	27/03/1916	27/03/1916
War Diary	Hulluch Sector South	28/03/1916	06/04/1916
War Diary	Lone Locality	07/04/1916	10/04/1916
War Diary	Hulluch Sector North	11/04/1916	19/04/1916
War Diary	Lone Locality	20/04/1916	22/04/1916
War Diary	Hulluch South	23/04/1916	30/04/1916
Heading	33rd Infantry Brigade 9th (S) Bn. The Sherwood Foresters. War Diary May 1918		
War Diary	Lone Locality	01/05/1918	02/05/1918
War Diary	Bracquemont	03/05/1918	09/05/1918
War Diary	St Elie N.	10/05/1918	18/05/1918
War Diary	Vermelles	19/05/1918	21/05/1918
War Diary	St Elie N.	22/05/1918	26/05/1918
War Diary	Braquemont	27/05/1918	03/06/1918
War Diary	Hay Locality	04/06/1918	07/06/1918
War Diary	Line Locality	08/06/1918	10/06/1918
War Diary	Posen Locality Chalk Pit	11/06/1918	19/06/1918
War Diary	Mazingarbe	20/06/1918	26/06/1918
War Diary	Right Bn Left Brigade	27/06/1918	30/06/1918
War Diary	9th Battalion The Sherwood War Diary For July 1918		
War Diary	St Elie Section	01/07/1918	13/07/1918
War Diary	Bois Du Froissart Near Hersin	14/07/1918	21/07/1918
War Diary	Hulluch Sector	21/07/1916	31/07/1916
War Diary	St Elie Sector	01/08/1918	05/08/1918
War Diary	Bracquemont	06/08/1918	25/08/1918
War Diary	Magnicourt	26/08/1918	29/08/1918
War Diary	Ecurie	30/08/1918	30/08/1918
War Diary	Trenches	31/08/1916	31/08/1916
Heading	9th Service Battalion The Sherwood Fusiliers War Diary For September 1918		
War Diary	Near Boiry Notre Dame	01/09/1918	07/09/1918
War Diary	Arras	08/09/1918	11/09/1918
War Diary	Boiry-Notre-Dame	12/09/1918	19/09/1918
War Diary	Feuchy	20/09/1918	20/09/1918
War Diary	Magnicourt	21/09/1918	21/09/1918
War Diary	Magnicourt En-Comte	24/09/1918	25/09/1918
War Diary	Vis-En-Artois	26/09/1918	27/09/1918

War Diary   Near Villers-Les-Cagnicourt   27/09/1918 30/09/1918

WO 95/25876

WAR DIARY
INTELLIGENCE SUMMARY
(Erase heading not required.)

Army Form C. 2118.

Instructions regarding War Diaries and Intelligence Summaries are contained in F. S. Regs., Part II. and the Staff Manual respectively. Title pages will be prepared in manuscript.

Place	Date	Hour	Summary of Events and Information	Remarks and references to Appendices
MAZINGARBE	January 1st 1918		Battalion in Reserve Billets. Company training & Organization of Working Parties. Battalion relieved 1/5 Suff. Regt in left sub sector without incident.	Annex II. 4p.m.
MAROC - LEFT SUB-SECTOR			Quiet day. Enemy rather active in front of Companies 95 R.R.	Vide info. attached
	3rd		Enemy put down Barrage on our Bat Front line, VENDIN, ALLEY & Reserve Line. No apparent loss.	
			Very quiet.	
	4th		Very quiet. Relief by 1/4th	
	5th		Very quiet.	
	6th		Situation normal. Enemy artillery very active on the ground batteries.	
	7th 6.15 a.m.		[illegible entries regarding officers and reliefs, names incl. BRENNAN, BANNATYNE, L.W. ESTER, TARNER, etc.]	
	8th 4 p.m.		Bn went to trenches at MAZINGARBE until Battalion relieved & returns to Reserve there.	
MAZINGARBE	10th		Batt relieved by 1st Leic. R. and marched back to Reserve. Leaving at about 9 p.m. and arriving about 2.30 a.m.	
	11th April		[illegible]	Annex II

Army Form C. 2118.

Instructions regarding War Diaries and Intelligence
Summaries are contained in F. S. Regs., Part II,
and the Staff Manual respectively. Title pages
will be prepared in manuscript.

WAR DIARY
or
INTELLIGENCE SUMMARY.
(Erase heading not required.)

Place	Date	Hour	Summary of Events and Information	Remarks and references to Appendices
Maggiore	13.7.18	11.30pm	Raid. 2 coys of S. Staffs on RIGHT sub-sector, 2 coys Sherwoods on LEFT sub-sector, 10 R.E. without ripdart, attacked by strength in line PO.KR. to R.V. R520. The enemy's forward positions were occupied	
HUNTERS RIDGE Sub-sector.	14th		Enemy artillery fire died down during morning opposite RGT.Cy. Day quiet	VIDE MAP A
"	15th		Enemy artillery hostile by night. Enemy artillery supported by one monitor	
"	16/7/18		Quiet day. S.O.S. company 10/13 took place in T.R.	
"	19		Enemy shelled Walpen Avenue. Our resources left nothing to be desired. He remained	
"	20th		Enemy reported to have occupied R236. Day of happened	
"	21st		Relief completed by Worcestershire Regt. moved into MAN RANGE	
MARTIN GARDEN	22nd		quiet day " " " " "	Jan 11
"	23rd		" " " H.Q.T.R. inspected prisoners	
"	"		from 11th Durt Regt.	
	24th		Company training rifle through enhances etc	

D. D. & L., London, E.C.
(A5883) Wt. W80/M672 350,000 4/17 Sch. 52a Forms/C/2118/14

Army Form C. 2118.

WAR DIARY
INTELLIGENCE SUMMARY.
(Erase heading not required.)

Instructions regarding War Diaries and Intelligence Summaries are contained in F. S. Regs., Part II. and the Staff Manual respectively. Title pages will be prepared in manuscript.

Place	Date	Hour	Summary of Events and Information	Remarks and references to Appendices
	February 1916			
Reinghelst	25th		Relieved 1st Bn Shropshire L.I. Bn HQ. behind Scottish Wood in J.33.c. Coys in King Post, Hole R.13. Post	
LEFT SUB-SECTOR "H"	26th		Day quiet. No casualties	Vide Map "H"
	27th	3 AM	Enemy attempt to raid our posts but were met by Lewis gun fire on Hedge Post. 3 casualties. Enemy thereupon quiet. 2 of our gun posts in squares B.23.c & d.	
	28th		Quiet day. Few enemy gun shells in square B.23.c & b. Our Batteries and T.M.'s engaged in bombarding at H.13.a. Bivouac & M. enemy wire in front.	6

Army Form C. 2118.

WAR DIARY
or
INTELLIGENCE SUMMARY.

(Erase heading not required.)

33rd Infantry Brigade.

9th Service Bn: The Sherwood Foresters.

War Diary.   March 1918.

Army Form C. 2118.

WAR DIARY
or
INTELLIGENCE SUMMARY.
(Erase heading not required.)

Instructions regarding War Diaries and Intelligence Summaries are contained in F. S. Regs., Part II. and the Staff Manual respectively. Title pages will be prepared in manuscript.

ORDERLY ROOM
9th SERVICE BATTALION
THE S. STAFFORD FORESTERS

Place	Date	Hour	Summary of Events and Information	Remarks and references to Appendices
Trenches	7/2/16		Key posted when company relief took place in daylight with the exception of Vendin Post.	
HULLUCH SECTOR NORTH	8th		Relieved very quiet. Garrison - N.L.F. ENT - general in trenches - no wire. Battalion relieved by 8th York Regt. and proceeded to reserve lines in NOEUX LES MINES	
"	6.F.	6pm	Bath, Leaving 40. Capestors. During the morning 2 of pts C. in ...	
MAZINGARBE	9/9/16		... O.O. T.B.B. Brigadier had pulse parade in Fuch Cin. Route to ...believe 9th Staff Regt in HULLUCH SECTOR - SOUTH. Relief complete 9.30 am occasional artillery.	
10th				
HULLUCH SECTOR SOUTH	11th		Quieter than last 48 hrs except patrolled by hostile aircraft. North and our own very active. Enemy aeroplane brought down easily, being seen by all officers and men in the centre.	
"	13th F	Noon 10+	Our advanced troops had enemy sniped on our left. Enemy worked quietly in. They had been very quiet. 3 of our left Enemy was	
			sending across he would not. .... Bombardment lasted from to 10.30pm. ...	
	13th			
			Quiet day. Some sniping. No unusual firing across. ...	
"	H" 11/6A.			
	16" F			

Army Form C. 2118.

WAR DIARY
INTELLIGENCE SUMMARY.
(Erase heading not required.)

Place	Date	Hour	Summary of Events and Information	Remarks and references to Appendices
HULLUCH SECTOR SUPPORT	17/5		Very quiet, working parties repairing Kinker salvage trench barricade. Night Disturbed. Shells exploding in English front line & Supp. trenches 9/10.	
"	18/5		Enemy threw up flares about daybreak. 9.23 bomb mortar & short 100 & 150-pr. mm shells to Pneumatics or changes. Enemy shrapnel fire.	
"	19/5		Day moderately quiet. Enemy gun fire on G.23b. Trip wire & wire.	
"	20/5		10 a.m. More gas shells on same locality. Heavy working parties.	
"	21/5		Heavy fire during night - Heavy M.G.G. S.A. Snipers, and M.M. sniping. 11 softest artillery from front of G.23. Enemy shrapnel shells south of 10 A.M.E.	
"	22 noon		Very quiet. Heavy bomb of M.25b on right. 11-1:30 to 4 heal shell bombardment held unseen by B.opers and Red 3 sections in places by 5.20 am call in.	
M[?] LANNOBE	23rd		Batts relieving.	
"	24th 5am		Sunday. Batts arrived been slept took tea of 17.00 p.m. Stept. Nando in relief at 9am in case of hostile enemy bombardment of BrigSS Ompt.	
"	25th 5am		Parade at 5am. Musketry, football match, drew k.R.R. Regt.	
"	26th 5am		Evening. Rained all afternoon, drawn.	
"	27/5		Parade 6 as on previous days.	
"			Evening & intercotony Loxing.	
			Orders to [?] into Lakins. into relief of Lcf Rgt who are away. Bat. Hd.Qr at Vermeules. 3 Coy 2 Coy in Left [?] new huts in north west.	

WAR DIARY
INTELLIGENCE SUMMARY

(Erase heading not required.)

Army Form C. 2118.

Place	Date	Hour	Summary of Events and Information	Remarks and references to Appendices
MESSINES SECTOR SOUTH	28/6		Bn. relieved 8th Yorks Regt. in trenches. Enemy's wire broken down by our 6" T.M.	
	29/6		Very quiet. Some working parties. Rather quiet night. Enemy's patrol met one of our night raiders 150 yds. S.E. of B9, which retired into enemy lines covered by rapid rifle fire & bombs.	
	30/6		Very quiet. Enemy's patrols were sent on to enemy trench but no movement seen except to S. of Messines.	
		3pm	Quiet. Arrangements made for a bombing raid on enemy between B9 & Shute Regt. Heavy T.M. gun fire from behind enemy lines seen about Messines.	
			Patrol work. Patrols went to enemy's front line ... ... Regt. Raid by 8th Yorks Regt. successful. Enemy state that enemy forces in the sector very small.	

WAR DIARY
INTELLIGENCE SUMMARY
(Erase heading not required.)

Army Form C. 2118.

Instructions regarding War Diaries and Intelligence Summaries are contained in F. S. Regs., Part II. and the Staff Manual respectively. Title pages will be prepared in manuscript.

Place	Date	Hour	Summary of Events and Information	Remarks and references to Appendices
HULLUCH SECTOR SOUTH	April 1st		Day quiet. Raid by 9th Lincoln Regt. which was to have taken place at 1 a.m. postponed until 2 a.m.	
	2nd	2am	Raiding party of 9th Lincoln Regt. moved out from our front line. Enemy snipers. 1 Offr. & 30 O.R.'s got to enemy loopholes & caused damage was very severe in enemy wire.	
		3pm	Heavy bombardment of our front line for 15 minutes. In retaliation enemy caused no damage. Trenches damage done to trenches & wire repaired during night.	
	3rd		Day quiet. Fighting patrols sent out during night. Usual work of improving and clearing trenches pursued.	
	4th		As in previous day.	
	5th		" " " Several bays of B Coy were to some extent of wire & wire in our own front line.	
	6th		Very Quiet. Relief by 9th R. Leicestr. Regt. and moved into billets in huts at 2 Bays in LONE TRENCH & 2 Bays in MAZINGARBE. Relief complete by midnight.	
LONE LOOP?? N.B.	7th		Day quiet. No other events. Working parties supplied. 19 P.C. & A Coy Rifle Range to billets 62 hours & 2 attached to working parties throughout, into enemy gas & behind Chateau. No very severe in No R. Coys.	
		1pm	Enemy resumes gas shelling. Continues until 8pm. Casualties rather heavy - some 15 to what was sent to Hospital.	
		9pm	18 P.C. Coy change over with A, B, C Coys in MAZINGARBE. Relief carried out without incident. Quiet during night.	
	8th	6am	Enemy recommences gas shelling. Continues until 11am. Our precautions taken & work undertaken. Practically no further casualties occur. Capt. & Capt. Hearns 2nd.	
			Slightly wounded in the hand but remains at duty.	

Army Form C. 2118.

WAR DIARY
INTELLIGENCE SUMMARY.
(Erase heading not required.)

Place	Date	Hour	Summary of Events and Information	Remarks and references to Appendices
LONE	April 10th		Day quiet. Enemy gun begins to shell spot on front & 2 rifles to reach sent to	
LOYALTY			patrol — One casualty. Started Wickness & Langritt.	
			Relies relief of Lincoln Regt of HULLUCH TUNNEL (NORTH JE2d) Relief complete by 10.30pm.	
		11.30pm	Without incident	
HULLUCH			Information received that Prussians opposite to Brewery in our 1st & 2nd G station in JAMES T.	
SECTOR			GIVENCHY area to enemy attack likely to extend to HULLUCH SECTOR on N/2 or 12/2.	
NORTH			Necessary precaution taken.	
	11th		Day quiet. Special work carried on by party preparing trenches to receive	
			hostile attack. Barricades new sap dug out during nights. B.C. in several trenches	
			R.E. and infantry patrols. Our Trench mortars active & did some work	
	12th		Day quiet. Patrols reported no formation of Prussian in front of position. Our Trench Mortars again very active. Artillery active on	
			our own side & elsewhere any movement & machine gun.	
			Intense harrassing fire on enemy trenches and communications.	
	13th 14th 15th		Weather fine. No enemy action taken place	
			All available men employed in digging strongholds & trenches, wire, improving	
	16th		Very quiet day. Lieut T. M. WILLYAMS S. with S. relieved by M. MOWATS Regt a relief completed by midnight. Lieut Vogt V.C. [?]	
	18th		on MOWATS relief. Midnight Lieut VOGT V.C. & 2nd German attack on Lone Rural.	
			Red British signals went during times to mortally hit & was repulsed on front	
	19th			

Army Form C. 2118.

WAR DIARY
or
INTELLIGENCE SUMMARY.
(Erase heading not required.)

Instructions regarding War Diaries and Intelligence Summaries are contained in F. S. Regs., Part II. and the Staff Manual respectively. Title pages will be prepared in manuscript.

Place	Date	Hour	Summary of Events and Information	Remarks and references to Appendices
LONE LOCALITY	7/1/16	20A	Heavy bombardment on left, NORTH of LA BASSEE CANAL. Our answering artillery fire at 7pm already noticed. On announcement made in early morning at our meeting in early front. Lt. Col. [illegible] can maintain at last minute from [illegible] self carried out without [illegible] us. Ms. Coy relieves G Coy. [illegible] respectively. The latter Coy proceed to MAINGARDE. [illegible]	
			Day quiet in Battn. Sect.	
		3.30-4.30pm 11.30pm	Heavy bombardment of hostile trenches from [illegible] carried on our right, but own enemy arrived in enemy front trench.	
	22nd	12 mid	Usual operations by night and machine gun fire activity. Pag. Battn. relieves 1/K. Lincolns Regt in WULVERGHEM South. Trench completed by 3.30am.	
WULVERGHEM SOUTH	23rd	2.30am	Entry into WULVERGHEM completed by 2.30 am. Quiet for 5 minutes and one shell wounded. A number of old time [illegible] from ration party near during the night. No casualties. No [illegible] required but No 2 Coy at request of O Coy loaned [illegible] [illegible] water cart to [illegible] as the peculiar arrangement by [illegible] this machine was not carried out.	
	24th		Quiet in morning – batten [illegible]	
			Enemy shell band [illegible] – MURRAY road. Every 71.31 from 8.10am – 9.30am. Enemy shells seen [illegible] from 1pm to 3.30am. Shrapnel shells in ROSS DUMP. Our guns replied.	
	25th			

Army Form C. 2118.

WAR DIARY
-or-
INTELLIGENCE SUMMARY.

(Erase heading not required.)

Instructions regarding War Diaries and Intelligence Summaries are contained in F. S. Regs., Part II. and the Staff Manual respectively. Title pages will be prepared in manuscript.

Place	Date	Hour	Summary of Events and Information	Remarks and references to Appendices
HULLUCH SOUTH.	April 26/15		Day quiet. Certain amount of enemy shells in front line and POSEN ALLEY and Juncture of POSEN DUMP and TENTH AVENUE. About 8.45 P.M.	
"	27/15	1/M	19th Bn. D. Artillery relieved 5th Army F.A. Bde. in his sector.	
"		2 am	Enemy burst of fire on our gas cylinders by shell fire, knocked pieces out and working party of "E" Coy. B Company. Views of standing and so oclock cancelled.	
"			Morning shelling of POSEN ALLEY during afternoon. Day quiet. Morning shelling of POSEN ALLEY during afternoon. Knocked no damage done.	
"		11.15 am	Standard on our right and enemy trenches. Little retaliation. but identifications secured.	
"	28/15		Quiet. Our field artillery active during morning. Enemy artillery active on LEFT RESERVE Coy. HQ. 4.5 to 5.9 and 4.2 during afternoon.	
"	29/15		Day quiet. Most enemy shelling of POSEN ALLEY during afternoon. Usual working parties & patrols & pieces work done strengthening & improving trenches and defences.	
"	30/15		Day quiet. Batn. relieved by 9th Staffs Regt. On relief 2nd R.W. Coy. 1 Cpl. & 2 Pts. + Batn HQ men into Bde. support to line trench, B Coy to billets in MAZINGARBE.	

33rd Infantry Brigade.

9th (S) Bn. The Sherwood Foresters.

War Diary.

May 1918.

Army Form C. 2118.

WAR DIARY
or
INTELLIGENCE SUMMARY.
(Erase heading not required.)

Instructions regarding War Diaries and Intelligence
Summaries are contained in F. S. Regs., Part II.
and the Staff Manual respectively. Title pages
will be prepared in manuscript.

Place	Date	Hour	Summary of Events and Information	Remarks and references to Appendices
LONE LOCALITY	1st		Enemy Artillery more active at night. [illegible] on Dunkirk	
			[illegible handwritten entries]	
	2nd		Battalion relieved by 1/3rd [illegible] Regt. [illegible]	
BRACQUEMONT	3rd		[illegible handwritten entry]	
	4th		Battalion less [illegible] [illegible] (Coy's) [illegible] at [illegible]	
			Weary up. [illegible] in [illegible]	
			[illegible] in the afternoon.	
	5th		Batln- now expected to [illegible] G.O.C. Division [illegible]	
			SERJt HUNT (M.M.) & PTE CLOWES (M.M.) C.O.'s congratulations [illegible]	
			[illegible handwritten entries]	

WAR DIARY
or
INTELLIGENCE SUMMARY

Place	Date	Hour	Summary of Events and Information	Remarks and references to Appendices
BRACQUEMONT	6-9		Training for the attack. Observed a Northern Survey Raid on Hulluch sector	
			fighting having brought back the prisoners & considerably higher	
			spirits in the men of the Bn. to be trained up to pitch of Keenness	
			30th January with Trench Mortars supported by Company Bn. Cdr. & were all.	
			Our own Bn. had erected reinforcements to trenches near critical way of	
			the sector held, was made by Company Ypres N. No.1.	490 1
ST ELIE N	10		Battalion relieved the 9th Welsh in the left sector of St	
			ELIE NORTH SECTOR Relief complete by 6pm	App 1. B
		11-12	Nor. S/L brought in from J.F.2.15 in STANSFIELD ROAD. The sanitary of area	
		6.30pm	The enemy artillery being very active. T.Ms. active throughout.	84.
			Hostile C.Bns shelled the right half of our front line at 7	
			10m Rifle shooting of the form seeing trouble severe amount	
			in time of the enemy died in Pretoria	
	13	1.30am	Gas bombardment on ST ELIE & FOSSE 8. Enemy shelling our line up to T.12	App C

Army Form C. 2118.

WAR DIARY
or
INTELLIGENCE SUMMARY.
(Erase heading not required.)

Place	Date	Hour	Summary of Events and Information	Remarks and references to Appendices
ST. ELIE N.	13.		[illegible - heavily scribbled out]	
	14.			
	15.1.			
	17.			

WAR DIARY or INTELLIGENCE SUMMARY

Army Form C. 2118.

Place	Date	Hour	Summary of Events and Information	Remarks and references to Appendices
ST. ELIE. N.	19.		Battalion returned to LEFT subsector of the Brigade front & by the R.S. Stafford Regt. & moved into Brigade support at VERMELLES. 3 Coys & the HQrs. of II. immediate vicinity & 1 Coy at LE RUTOIRE FARM. (Approx: to be taken up later will be sent to the Army Comm. the 11th Manch. Mess or on Orderly Duty station)	209. E
		7.30am	11th Manchester Regt. & 33 Brigade made enemy third line (HILD TRENCH) between H.13.c.9.1.13. & H.13.c.20.88. Rather now occupied an advance LHS trench from H.13.c.9.1.13. & H.13.c.20.88. Rather dug-outs in identification & did considerable damage to material. Several bombs and known dead.	226. F.
VERMELLES	19 to 21.		During this period the Battalion took no active part in operations. Bosche shelled intermittently using "Blue Cross" shell & occasional gas & more Tear-Gas shells but not causing any damage.	213.
ST. ELIE. N.	22.		Battalion relieved 6th Lincoln Regt. in front line. Relief completed by 5 p.m.	April. G.
	23.		Enemy gas cylinders were discharged at 10.30 p.m.	
	24.	12.30am	Raid was carried out by N.R.R.C. on the front of the 1st Division on our LEFT. There was some retaliation on our sector. 11 Prisoners were captured. Several men in our company post T.M.B. Projectors were discharged in Divisional front & enemy retaliated strongly.	
		11 p.m	7 Lt. C.S. BULL was again wounded.	
	25.		Battalion relieved by 11th Manchester Regt. & moved into billets at BRACQUEMONT.	
	26.		Also 3.3 Brigade going into Divisional Reserve. All ranks were employed in getting into baths & cleaning up.	Ow. H.

WAR DIARY
or
INTELLIGENCE SUMMARY.

Army Form C. 2118.

Place	Date	Hour	Summary of Events and Information	Remarks and references to Appendices
BRAQUEMONT	27.		Day devoted to Bathing, Refitting of Clothes & Cleaning up.	
	28.		Battalion busied in starting & improving accommodation.	
	29.		[illegible - struck through]	
	30.		[illegible - struck through]	
	31.		[illegible - struck through]	

A.E. Leslie
LIEUT-COLONEL
COMDG. 9th SERVICE Bn. THE SHERWOOD FORESTERS

WAR DIARY
or
INTELLIGENCE SUMMARY
(Erase heading not required.)

Army Form C. 2118.

Place	Date	Hour	Summary of Events and Information	Remarks and references to Appendices
BRACQUEMONT	1918 June 1st	—	The Battn. at rest. Football Match against 6th LINCOLNS. Result, Lost 2-0	
"	2nd	—	Church Parade. Inter. Platoon Football Matches in the afternoon	
"	3rd	—	The Battn. left BRACQUEMONT 9 p.m. & relieved 6th Gord. & Lanc. in MAY LOCALITY. Left Sect. Sector of Right Brigade. B. "B" Co. at MAZINGARBE. Echelon at HERSIN	See Appx No. 1 See Appx No. 2
May Locality	4th	—	Relief complete 1 a.m. Sector heavily shelled from 2 till 3 am. 4 Cleneleus "A" Co. Raid by 9th ROYAL SUSSEX, 73rd Inf. Bde. on our right at H.6.6.d. 3/5 11.15 pm. Two prisoners captured.	
"	5th	—	Fairly heavy shelling from 10 to 11 pm, including a hide missed Gas	

Army Form C. 2118.

WAR DIARY
or
INTELLIGENCE SUMMARY.
(Erase heading not required.)

Instructions regarding War Diaries and Intelligence Summaries are contained in F. S. Regs., Part II. and the Staff Manual respectively. Title pages will be prepared in manuscript.

Place	Date	Hour	Summary of Events and Information	Remarks and references to Appendices
Hay Locality	6th June /18	—	On the night of the 6/7th the Boundary between the Right & Right Brigade in the Divisional Sector was altered & the Boundary in the RESERVE LINE between the Right & Left Batt of the Right Brigade was altered.	See appen No. 113 See Map No. 1
"	7th	—	On the night of the 7/8th the Batt (less "B" Co.) was relieved on the Left Sub Section of the Brigade Front by the 9 L. STAFFS. Dispositions as follows:— Bn. H.Q. B Co. C Co. D Co. HOUSONS POST. MAZINGARBE (Southern part) LONE TRENCH TENTH AVENUE.	See appen No. 4
Lone trench	8th	—	At 12.30 a.m. Gas Projectors were projected from G.20.1/2; G.11.d.9.9/3.5 G.11.d.25/10.5 on the NORTHUMBERLAND FUSILIERS front 3rd Brigade. Retaliation on our Sector was slight.	See appen No. 5 See Map No. 1
"	9th	—	A.C. from MAZINGARBE relieved C Co. in DUFFERS DRIFT (LONE TR)	See appen No. 6

Army Form C. 2118.

WAR DIARY
or
INTELLIGENCE SUMMARY.
(Erase heading not required.)

Instructions regarding War Diaries and Intelligence Summaries are contained in F. S. Regs., Part II. and the Staff Manual respectively. Title pages will be prepared in manuscript.

Place	Date	Hour	Summary of Events and Information	Remarks and references to Appendices
In trenches	1918 Jan 10th	1 a.m.	A special Gas Cylinder operation took place on our Right (24th Div). Cylinders of a new type being discharged. Retaliation on our Front nil.	See Appendix No. 7
From Locality "A" to R.R.Pt "B"	11th		The Bakers (less B Co) relieved three Companies of the 6th LINCS in the Right Sub Section of the Brigade Front. Relief complete at 11 p.m.	See Appx No. 8 See pg No. 1.
"	12		Nothing unusual.	
"	13		Nothing unusual.	
"	14	12.15 p.m.	A second Mortar Gas operation took place on the Front of the Brigade on our Left. Retaliation was heavy on RESERVE LINE, N. of VENDIN ALLEY (C Co's Front.)	See Appx No. 9

WAR DIARY
OF
INTELLIGENCE SUMMARY.
(Erase heading not required.)

Army Form C. 2118.

Place	Date	Hour	Summary of Events and Information	Remarks and references to Appendices
	1918 June 15		The 6th LINCS relieved the 7th SSTAFFS in the Left Sub-Section on the night of the 15/16th	See Appx No. 13
		6pm	Pt. J. Seker, a nigger (a 15cm shell from C.C.H.Q. which to be away O.C. for our E. We had people left B.H.Q. after the C.O's Conference.	See Appx No. 1.
		6pm till 8pm	7th Junction of RESERVE LINE & VENDIN MULEY was heavily shelled with 15cm. Three casualties in addition to O.R. Killed. (2 killed, 1 wounded)	
16th			B.C. + 10, 30 O.R. C.Co. joined the Raid in the line from MAZINGARBE during the evening	
17th		6pm	The 73rd Inf Brigade on our Right carried out a Raid, meeting on one prisoner being captured. Retaliation on our front was slight.	See Appx No. 14
	18th	7am	Five Officers & 160 O.R's of the Battn (4 O's + 130 O.R's from "B" Co. + 1 O. + 30 O.R's from "C" Co.) carried out a Raid on the enemy lines in H.25 C. 59.68 & H.19 al. 27. 25. resulting in the capture of 7 Prisoners & 1 Machine Gun. The Officers who took part were :—	See Appx No. 14 See App No. 7.

WAR DIARY
INTELLIGENCE SUMMARY.
(Erase heading not required.)

Army Form C. 2118.

Place	Date 1915	Hour	Summary of Events and Information	Remarks and references to Appendices
"	June 18 (Cont)		Capt. H.C.T. Wainfore M.C. (O.C. Raid) "B" Co. 2/Lt. F.J. Forrest 2/Lt. J.R.B. Kilner 2/Lt. W.E. Thorborn 2/Lt. B.S. Parker "C" Co. Our Casualties were:- 1 Officer killed 2/Lt Kilner 1 " missing believed killed 2/Lt Thorborn 3 O.R.s killed 1 " missing believed killed 11 " Wounded 1 " Wounded & missing. The Raiding Party returned to MAZINGARBE during the evening.	See Appen. No. 15
		11.30 pm.	Gas Projectors were projected from S.11 c 3.7; S.18 c 77 & S.11 & 4.5. Retaliation on our Lines was rather heavy.	See Appen No. 16 See Page No. 1

Army Form C. 2118.

WAR DIARY
INTELLIGENCE SUMMARY.
(Erase heading not required.)

Instructions regarding War Diaries and Intelligence Summaries are contained in F. S. Regs., Part II. and the Staff Manual respectively. Title pages will be prepared in manuscript.

Place	Date	Hour	Summary of Events and Information	Remarks and references to Appendices
	1914 June 19		Major E.L. Hoskins M.C. sent to hospital with influenza. On the night of the 19th/20th the Batt. was relieved by the 11th MANCHESTER REGT. 3rd Brigade, & proceeded to Red Billets in MAZINGARBE for 8 days. Relief complete about 2 am 20th.	See appx. 1/5.13
MAZINGARBE	20th	6pm	Companies Bathing & Cleaning up. The 3rd F.A.B. band from the Remainder of Captain's Infantry Brigade gave a Concert to the Bagn. in the Divisional theatre	
	21st	9am tea 2.30pm	Companies training. Recreational training in the afternoon	
"		6pm	Cinema at Div.l theatre. Lt. Royle (Med. Offr.) slightly wounded during shelling of the AVENUE. A party of B.H.Q. been over hit. Capt. A.E. Brennan (B.Co) assumes duty of 2/Command. Garrison Orders in case of hostile aircraft issued	See appx. No 12

Army Form C. 2118.

WAR DIARY
INTELLIGENCE SUMMARY.
(Erase heading not required.)

Instructions regarding War Diaries and Intelligence Summaries are contained in F. S. Regs., Part II. and the Staff Manual respectively. Title pages will be prepared in manuscript.

Place	Date	Hour	Summary of Events and Information	Remarks and references to Appendices
MAZINGARBE	1918 June 22nd	9 a.m. 12:30 pm	Companies training "A" & "C" Coys. carry out firing Exercises on Range. Recreational training in the afternoon.	
		6 pm	Cinema at Divisional Theatre. Pte. Alexander (M.O.) commenced leave to England, relieved by Capt. Lowrie, 3rd F.A. Lt. Roy C. sent to Hospital.	
"	23rd		Church Parades. D Coy. carry out firing Exercises on Range. Swimming Competition in afternoon.	
"	24th	6 pm	The Battn. on Field Day. Tactical Exercise. Bn operation between infantry & tanks carried out near AIX NOULETTE. (R27 central) Cinema at Divisional Theatre.	

Army Form C. 2118.

WAR DIARY
of
INTELLIGENCE SUMMARY.
(Erase heading not required.)

Instructions regarding War Diaries and Intelligence Summaries are contained in F. S. Regs., Part II. and the Staff Manual respectively. Title pages will be prepared in manuscript.

Place	Date	Hour	Summary of Events and Information	Remarks and references to Appendices
MAZINGARBE	1918 June 25th	9am to 12.30pm	Companies Training & G.O's inspection	
		3 pm	Swimming Competition	
		6 pm	Cinema at Divil Theatre	
"	26th	9am to 12.30pm	Companies Training	
		6 pm	Cinema at Divil Theatre	
Right Bn. Left Brigade	27th	2.30pm	The Batt. left MAZINGARBE & proceeded to the Right Sub-Sector of the ST. ELIE Section, relieving the 2nd Yorks. Relief complete at 6 pm. Major Myers commences leave to England.	See Appx No. 17 See Page No. 1
"	28th		A Co. Sector (DEVON LANE - ST. MARY'S DUMP) heavily shelled with 10 & 15 cm. in the afternoon. Two Casualties (wounded)	

Army Form C. 2118.

WAR DIARY
or
INTELLIGENCE SUMMARY.
(Erase heading not required.)

Instructions regarding War Diaries and Intelligence Summaries are contained in F. S. Regs., Part II. and the Staff Manual respectively. Title pages will be prepared in manuscript.

Place	Date	Hour	Summary of Events and Information	Remarks and references to Appendices
	1918			
RIGHT BN	June 29	10 AM	11th Divl. Horse Show was held at Q.16.b.40.00. 3 officers & about 6 ORs proceeded there from the line, returning the same night. Two prizes were won on the first day by the Bn. 2nd in Class IV. Yeo. int (Individual) Mounted. Corp. Wright representing the Battn.	Sheet 44B.
LEFT BDE.		4 pm	Holmes XI 2nd Large Infantry Heavy-draught Horse.	See appendix no. 19.
			Reinforcement which arrived at London on the 27th joined the Bn up the line on the night of the 28th Sept.	
	June 30		2nd day of the Divl. Horse Show	
			2nd Lieut. F.A. ALLEN went down from the line to proceed on a 2 days course on Camouflage, to BOULOGNE.	

H. Cloathen Lt Col.
Cmdg 9th Munster Fusiliers.

Army Form C. 2118.

WAR DIARY
or
INTELLIGENCE SUMMARY.

(Erase heading not required.)

9th Battalion. The Norfolk Fusiliers

War Diary

July 1918

Army Form C. 2118.

WAR DIARY
or
INTELLIGENCE SUMMARY.
(Erase heading not required.)

Instructions regarding War Diaries and Intelligence Summaries are contained in F. S. Regs., Part II. and the Staff Manual respectively. Title pages will be prepared in manuscript.

Place	Date	Hour	Summary of Events and Information	Remarks and references to Appendices
ST. ELIE SECTION	1915 July		The Batt. was relieved in the Right Sub-Sector of the Brigade Front by the 6th Lincolnshires in the afternoon & proceeded as follows:—	See Appx No. 20
			Bn. H.Q. . . . . . VERMELLES BREWERY.	
			A Co. . . . . . VERMELLES NORTH	
			B Co. . . . . . MAZINGARBE	
			C Co. . . . . . VERMELLES SOUTH	
			D Co. . . . . . CROSSWAY	
			The Batt. in Support.	
	3		Companies Bathing at Baths in NOYELLES & MAZINGARBE. Enemy Artillery was quiet during the period. Extracts from London Gazette dated June 27th 1918. "Capt. (acting-Major) C.R. Harding, M.C. to be Temporary Major July 29th 1917." "Sergt./Sec. Lt. S. Albouchement relinquishes acting rank of Captain on ceasing to command a Co. 24th Oct. 1918." The following were awarded the M.M. in connection with the Raid on June 18 :—	See Appx No. 1 of JUNE
	3		Sgt. P. Griffin. Pte W. Sulley. Sgt. J. R. Lee. Sgt. R. Greer was awarded a Bar to his M.M.	

Army Form C. 2118.

WAR DIARY
of
INTELLIGENCE SUMMARY.
(Erase heading not required.)

Instructions regarding War Diaries and Intelligence Summaries are contained in F. S. Regs., Part II. and the Staff Manual respectively. Title pages will be prepared in manuscript.

Place	Date	Hour	Summary of Events and Information	Remarks and references to Appendices
	1915			
	July 2nd		For the purpose of carrying out a scheme of communication	
	3rd		telephones or telegraphones have been used from 3 am to 8 am at	
	4th			
	(Cont'd)			
	5th	2pm	The Batt. relieved the 7th S. Staffs in the left sub sector of the	See Appx
			"Bois" was disposed as follows:	No. 21
			ST ELIS SECTION . . . . . CHAPEL ALLEY	See Appx
			Bn H.Q . . . . GORDON Co	No. 1 of
			A Co	JUNE
			B Co . . . . STANSFIELD Co	
			C Co . . . . MANNING Co	
			D Co . . . . STUDIO Co	
			Operation Order No. 50 re Roan Sur Ronche issued	See Appx
				No. 22
	6th			
	7th		Nothing Remarkable	
			2nd Lt. Rigden D Co proceeded on leave to England	
	8th		2nd Lieut. Percival A Co proceeded to Rest Camp near BOULOGNE	

Army Form C. 2118.

WAR DIARY
or
INTELLIGENCE SUMMARY.
(Erase heading not required.)

Instructions regarding War Diaries and Intelligence Summaries are contained in F. S. Regs., Part II. and the Staff Manual respectively. Title pages will be prepared in manuscript.

Place	Date	Hour	Summary of Events and Information	Remarks and references to Appendices
	1918 July 9th	9ᵃ	"C" CO. (MANNING CO) relieved "D" CO (STUDIO CO) during the afternoon. The 7 S. STAFFS relieved the 6TH LINCS in the Right Sub. Section of ST. ELIE SECTION during the afternoon.	See Appen No. 23. See Appen No. 24
		10ᵗʰ	Capt H.V.C. WARNEFORD, M.C. left the Bn. & proceeded to 59ᵗʰ DIV to assist in training (temporarily)	
		11ᵗʰ	Contact Signalling was arranged to take place during the morning between the Bn. Signallers & a Contact Aeroplane but the aeroplane was forced to descend behind our Lines owing to Engine trouble. Operation Order No.58 re Establishment of Bn. Objectors at E.O.H.C. 307 & G.11.d.m.5. issued.	See Appen No. 25 See Appen No. 1 of JUNE
		12ᵗʰ	Major C.L. HARDING, M.C. returns to the Bn. from Convalescence. Right Bn. Defence Scheme (ST. ELIE SECTION) issued.	See Appen No. 26
		13ᵗʰ	On the night of the 12/13. a Raiding Party broken down in the Dail & Brunet (on our Right) the Ens. was discovered from shelters on the 9th. back at about G.172.9.1. + G.29.a 2.6. The only retaliation on our sector was a few 77 Gas on the HAIRPINS fired by C. Co. (STUDIO CO)	See Appen No. 22

Army Form C. 2118.

WAR DIARY
or
INTELLIGENCE SUMMARY.
(Erase heading not required.)

Instructions regarding War Diaries and Intelligence Summaries are contained in F. S. Regs., Part II. and the Staff Manual respectively. Title pages will be prepared in manuscript.

Place	Date	Hour	Summary of Events and Information	Remarks and references to Appendices
	1918 Feb. 13 (cont)		The Batt. was relieved by the 8th NUMBERLD FUSILIERS (34th Brigade) during the afternoon. Enemy shelled tracks near MAZINGARBE at 7.30 p.m. & damaged the Batt. to the Wind Camp at BOIS DU FROISSART. The Relief was completed at 9.00 p.m.	See Appx No. 3
BOIS DU FROISSART NEAR HERSIN.	14th		The Batt. out for 8 days rest. Companies occupy gym & baths.	
		2.30 pm	Cricket Match Senior v Junior Officers. The Seniors winning. Score 80 - 48. Capt. A.E. BRENNAN relinquishes position of Act/2/Command in Major C. HARDING. M.C. returning from Leave.	
	15th	9 am 12.30 pm	Companies training in Basketry. P.T. & B.F. Lieut. McCORMICK, 2nd Lieut. Cross Inter Duet & successful found. Officers meeting held in the afternoon conducted by Col. T.O. Pte BUGDEN SMITH.	See Appx No. 25
		6 pm	Trophies March Lost Base v 50th F.A.B. and 1 - 0. Batt. Band played during the evening. The Supper in Apparatus. Defeat & Scheme issued.	See Appx No. 29

Army Form C. 2118.

WAR DIARY
INTELLIGENCE SUMMARY.
(Erase heading not required.)

Instructions regarding War Diaries and Intelligence Summaries are contained in F. S. Regs., Part II. and the Staff Manual respectively. Title pages will be prepared in manuscript.

Place	Date	Hour	Summary of Events and Information	Remarks and references to Appendices
	1918 July 16th	9 am to 12.30 pm	Company training as usual	
		2 pm	Tactical Exercise for Officers under Major PIPER	
			Recreational training in afternoon (Cricket & Rounders)	
			Draft of 11 O.R's arrived	
	17th		Withdrawal scheme carried out by the Bn - near BOUVIGNY - BOYEFFLES Rifle Camps at 7.30 am. Operations 2pm. The Divisional General was present.	
		2.30 pm	Creech Mount on Camp-ground. The Band & 12 Shenwood Foresters Bench Band dug for 105 a.m. — 2nd/Lt. F.S. PARKER (C Co) returned the M.C. & Co Sgt Major S.C. LEE (B Co) the D.C.M. in connect[ion] with raid of 18 June.	
	18th	9 am	Batt Rifle Meeting was held on the Range at O 2 in near the Camp, commencing at 9 am	See System No. 31
			EVENTS (1) Falling plate competition (2) Team Competition practices. Give mounds applicable in, 200 yds 15 rounds in one minute at 300 yds. Bayonet point to swords empl Shooting at 300 yds enthusiastic target.	

WAR DIARY
INTELLIGENCE SUMMARY
(Erase heading not required.)

Army Form C. 2118.

Place	Date	Hour	Summary of Events and Information	Remarks and references to Appendices

1918 July 18 (cont.)

(3) Co. for N.C.O. Officer & Warrant Officer rifles
(4) Individual magazine of 5 rounds at 200 yds. aluminium target
(5) Rapid shoot, 2 chargers, firing at 300 yds
(6) Snap shoot, 200 yds at moving man
(7) Gas helmet shoot

WINNERS

EVENT
(1) Bn. N.Q.
(2) C Co.
(3) W.O.'s & Sgts.
(4) L/Cpl W. UPTON, C Co. 1st
     Pte. J. WAGSTAFFE, M.O. 2nd
     L/Cpl SHAW. 3rd)
     C Co.) 3rd
     Pte G. BEAT.

EVENT
5) Pte S. STUART C Co.
6) Pte W. MUGGLETON'S C Co.
7) 2nd Lt. W. FOSTER, H.Q. 1st
   Pte V. WILLIS C Co.
   Capt. F. BARRETT M.O.) 2nd
   Pte G. H. LEAR M.O.) 2nd
   Pte C. CARRINE C Co.

Total Prizes   B.H.Q. 24½; C Co. 20½; B Co. 2

The Divl. Boxing competition held at the Divl. Recreation Camp. COURIGNY commenced at 11 am. Knock-out tournament for 3 days. Officers were granted leave from the Bn.

* 2/Lt H. FRANCIS, B Co. proceeded on leave under PARIS Leave arrangement.

Army Form C. 2118.

WAR DIARY
or
INTELLIGENCE SUMMARY.
(Erase heading not required.)

Place	Date	Hour	Summary of Events and Information	Remarks and references to Appendices
	1918 July 18		2/Lieut J.S. Williams, C Co left the Bn & proceeded to the M.G. School at GRANTHAM	
	1918 July 19		2nd Stage of Bn Boxing Competition. Companies carried out Firing Practice on the Range from 9am - 2pm. Officers Riding Class in the afternoon. Preliminary heats run in Bn Sports in the evening	
	1918 July 20		The Divl Commander (Maj Genl Davies) accompanied by the Brigade Commander (Brig Gen Spooner) inspected the Bn on the Bomb Attack Ground at 10am & afterwards presented Ribbons to the following for gallantry during the raid of the 15th of June last. 2/Lieut J.S. Paxton M.C. C.S.M. S.E. Lee D.C.M. Sergt R. Tees M.M. Bar to M.M. L/C P. Griffin M.M. Pte J.O. Lee M.M. Pte W.J. Sulley M.M.	550

WAR DIARY
or
INTELLIGENCE SUMMARY

Army Form C. 2118.

Place	Date	Hour	Summary of Events and Information	Remarks and references to Appendices
	1918 20 July cont'd		9/ Lieut Whitt A.C. proceeds on leave with PARIS Wed 24 Aug next.	
			Major C.L. Harding M.C. will be attached to 6" York & Lancs 32nd Brigade as from this date.	See Appen N° 32
			The following Sports took place in the Bois du FROISSART.	
			EVENTS	
			i. Final 440 yds	
			ii. Sack Race in gas helmets.	
			iii. 1/4 mile.	
			iv. Drill Blindfolded	
			v. Final 100 yds	
			vi. Obstacle Race	
			vii. Final Tug-of-War	
			viii. Relay Race	
			ix. Bun, Biscuit & whistle race	
			Much Joviality was carried out throughout the sports.	

WAR DIARY
or
INTELLIGENCE SUMMARY.

Army Form C. 2118.

Place	Date	Hour	Summary of Events and Information	Remarks and references to Appendices
	1918 31 July		Church Parades	
			Companies bathed at HERSIN baths	
			Extract from Battalion Orders	
			Divisional Boxing Tournament	See Appx No 33
			The Commanding Officer congratulates Sgt Sheppard (on winning the Welterweight Championship) of the Battalion	
			The Battalion was the top of the 64th Brigade with 13 points	
			Note. The Battalion relieved the 9th HULLUCH Sector today	
HULLUCH SECTOR			The Battalion relieved the 9th "WEST YORKSHIRE REST in SUPPORT in the HULLUCH	
			D Coy Sherwood Foresters relieved B Coy 9" W Yorks in TENTH AVENUE	See Map
			D " " " D " " " LONE TRENCH (Buffers Left)	of
			B " " " A " " " NORTHERN HUTS MAZINGARBE	
			A " " " " " " Do	
			C " " " C " " "	
			A & C Coys marched to MAZINGARBE	
			B & D " were conveyed in lorries	
			Battalion moved to Divn Reception Camp at BOURISNY	

Army Form C. 2118.

WAR DIARY
or
INTELLIGENCE SUMMARY.
(Erase heading not required.)

Instructions regarding War Diaries and Intelligence Summaries are contained in F. S. Regs., Part II. and the Staff Manual respectively. Title pages will be prepared in manuscript.

Place	Date	Hour	Summary of Events and Information	Remarks and references to Appendices
	1918			
	21 July cont.		Capt W Mason (Int Off) proceeded to 33rd Bde H.Q. for ~~instructional purposes approx~~ 10 Days duty. 2nd Lt M Hansman proceeded to PARIS-PLAGE for 10 days rest	
	22nd		Nothing Unusual. Capt W Mason proceeded to 33 Inf Bde as understudy to Staff Captain	
	23		Companies training. A trial match Sherwood Foresters v 2 Yorkshire Reg¹ was played on the LES BRÉBIS football field. Result - Sh Foresters 69 runs, York. Regt. 58.	
	24		Companies in RESERVE continued their training	

WAR DIARY
or
INTELLIGENCE SUMMARY.

(Erase heading not required.)

Army Form C. 2118.

Place	Date	Hour	Summary of Events and Information	Remarks and references to Appendices
HULLUCH SECTOR	25th		The Bn relieved the 1/ "South Stafford Regt" in the Right Sub Sector.	
			"D" Co 9th Sher Foresters relieved "C" Coy 1/ S Staff CHALK PIT COMPANY	Sn 4FA 34
			"D" " " " " " " "D" " " " POSEN COMPANY	
			"B" " " " " " " "B" " " " BROADWAY "	
			"C" " " " " " " "A" " " "	
			"A" " " " " " " "G" " " " ESSEX COMPANY	
			Battalion Hd Qrs in CURZON STREET "	
			Relief completed by 11.30 pm.	
			Extract from Operation Order No 105	
			N° 4 Section Special Company R.E. will carry out Sn 4FA a Gas & trench Mortar bombardment of the hostile trenches W of HULLUCH on the night of the 25/26/17/1915 if weather conditions are favourable.	35

(A7092) Wt W12859/M1293. 75,000. 1/17. D. D. & L., Ltd. Forms/C.2118/14.

WAR DIARY
or
INTELLIGENCE SUMMARY.

(Erase heading not required.)

Army Form C. 2118.

Place	Date	Hour	Summary of Events and Information	Remarks and references to Appendices
	25"			
	6nd 24		No of Guns Emplacements Targets Fuzes	See over
			5 Q.18.d.95-80 HOUZZA TRENCH T.M.B.	
			H.13.d.35.99 No 120	
			H.13.d.13/88 P.S.30.	
			All mortars of ESSEX COMPANY and those the maximum number of shells to fall in each case on each supposed by Z.500 minus 5 minutes.	
			The operation will be controlled by the following code	
			Cros will be fired 12.9.M GLAD	
			DATUM being 11pm. Zero will be DATUM plus 3. (i.e. 2.6 am)	
			Operation cancelled GLOOM	
			" successful + all clear GL GAY	
			GLEE	
			ZERO postponed 2 hours	
	26		The above bombardment mentioned yesterday was successfully carried out this morning at 2am. Retaliation was slight.	

WAR DIARY
or
INTELLIGENCE SUMMARY.
(Erase heading not required.)

Army Form C. 2118.

Place	Date	Hour	Summary of Events and Information	Remarks and references to Appendices
	27		Nothing unusual	
	28		LT. BOWYER proceeded on leave to ENGLAND. A barrage of 152m shells was put down on ESSEX COMPANY (C.154d) at 1.15pm. Wire cutting and destructive shoots were carried out by 4 & 6" Hows & 6" TM's on enemy M.G. emplts with good results.	See Appx.
	29		The barrage mentioned yesterday was repeated this morning at 11am at the same gas shells were fired on enemy M.Gs at H.20.b.2.5.5.	
	30		Nothing unusual	
	31		Nothing unusual	A.J. [signature]

Army Form C. 2118.

WAR DIARY
of
INTELLIGENCE SUMMARY.
(Erase heading not required.)

Place	Date	Hour	Summary of Events and Information	Remarks and references to Appendices
ST ELIE SECTOR	Aug 1918 1st		Capt WARNEFORD, M.C. (B Coy) proceeded to ENGLAND for 6 months' duty at home under the Liberalisa scheme. 2/Lt TOOKE proceeded to 1st CORPS M.O. for several days.	
	2nd		The Batt" was relieved in the Right Sub Sector by the 6th LINC Regiment the afternoon proceeded as follows:-	Rev Appen No. 36
		2pm	B + D Coy ... NORTHERN HUTS, MAZINGARBE	
			"A" Coy TENTH AVENUE	
			"C" Coy DUFFERS DRIFT	
		7pm	B H Q HOWSONS POINT	
	3rd		Nothing to record.	
	4th		A party of 25 ORs under 2/Lt PERCIVAL, proceeded to RANCHICOURT by lorry in order to represent the Batt" on the 1st Army Commemoration leave in France on the anniversary of our entry into the war.	
		11.30pm	A gas projector bombardment followed at 2ays + 35 + beyond by a shrapnel barrage was directed against the enemy's line opposite FOSSE 8 (A5a + 6) Retaliation was slight.	Rev Appen No. 36 A

25.2

Army Form C. 2118.

WAR DIARY
or
INTELLIGENCE SUMMARY.
(Erase heading not required.)

Instructions regarding War Diaries and Intelligence Summaries are contained in F. S. Regs., Part II. and the Staff Manual respectively. Title pages will be prepared in manuscript.

Place	Date	Hour	Summary of Events and Information	Remarks and references to Appendices
	Aug 1		Nothing unusual	
	5th		The Battn. was relieved by the 8th N.F.'s & proceeded to Rest Billets at the Egypt	
	6th		BRACQUEMONT for 8 days. The relief was complete by 7 pm	No. 37
BRACQUE-MONT	7th		Companies bathing & cleaning up	
	8th		The Battn. (less A Co) carried out Rest Divnl. Training Practices on the Training Ground in R3d (Sheet 44 & 1/4000) Series of march moving off at 8 am. Bn. H.Q., Band, B, C, & D Coys. Dinner was served on the ground & the Battn. returned to billets at 5.30 pm A. Co. fired the following Practices on the GARRISON Range from 2–5 pm. 5 rds application at 200 yds. 15 rds rapid at 300 yds. 5 " " " 200 " 5 " "snapshooting" " 10 " " " The following Officers appeared on Ration Orders:- 2/Lt S MAISHMENT taken over B.C. 9-7.9.18. w.e.f. 5.9.18. McKINRYFORD M.C. LT C.R.T. WILMOT taken over C. Co. vice Capt CHORLTON 7/9/18 LT R.W. BOWYER 2/Lt A.C. 7/9/18 LT CARTLEDGE 7/9/18 O.C. 7/9/18 2/Lt HETHERINGTON 7/9/18 B.C. 7/9/1918 Capt CHARLTON 7/9/18 D.S. 2/LT. COOPER R. to Rest. Egypt	

WAR DIARY
INTELLIGENCE SUMMARY

Army Form C. 2118.

Place	Date	Hour	Summary of Events and Information	Remarks and references to Appendices
BRACQUEMONT	Aug 13	9am to 12.30pm	Company Training. Musketry PT & BF. Close Order Drill &c. Greneades, tonitig.	
			Recreational training in afternoon (Cricket Hockey)	
	10th	9.11.30 am	BOIS DU FROISSART range was inspected to the Barr as follows :- B Co. 11.30am - 2pm C Co. The following particulars were furnish :- 5. No. applications at 200 yds. 200 yds 15 " rapid , 200 yds 5 " snapshooting	
		11am to 2.30pm	Junior NCO's Class (8 per Co) under RSM	
		11am	Officers killed exercise (3 per Co) under Major PIPER. A & D Co's training as usual. The following matches were played in the afternoon. Hockey Bn V 6/LINCS at BRACQUEMONT Result Bn won 3-1. Soccer Bn V 6/LINCS at MAZINGARBE Result Bn lost 1-4	
			Capt A.E.BRENDAN proceeded on leave to ENGLAND	
			Enemy aircraft dropped about 60 bombs in vicinity of BRACQUEMONT - NOEUX-LES-MINES between 11pm - 2 am. (U.K.)	

Army Form C. 2118.

WAR DIARY
or
INTELLIGENCE SUMMARY.
(Erase heading not required.)

Instructions regarding War Diaries and Intelligence Summaries are contained in F. S. Regs., Part II. and the Staff Manual respectively. Title pages will be prepared in manuscript.

Place	Date	Hour	Summary of Events and Information	Remarks and references to Appendices
BRACQUEMONT	Aug 11	10.30am	Church service at Div HQrs. A.C. Smt preached.	
		10am to 3pm	Vicinity of MONUMENT, NOEUX-LES-MINES + MAZINGARBE shelled with 4.2" + 5.9". A free service which should have been given to the Bn by 1st Div Concert Party in the PATRONAGE, NOEUX-LES-MINES, was postponed owing to the Hall being hit during the shelling. 1st Bn played 8/41 MGC at tennis at MAZINGARBE. Bn lost. There was some mowing bombing by the enemy during the night.	
	12th	9pm to 12.35pm	Companies training, including Returns to Bato+s by their Comma2nd 2/Lt OSBORNE proceeded to Rest Camp & AIRE thru PARIS-PLAGE.	
	13	9am to 12.30p	Training continues. Platoons as disposal of their Company officers. Shelling of NOEUX-les-MINES repeated. Draft details for Gas test Gamp received and sent on Brass Band.	
	14	5.30p	Shelling of NOEUX-les-MINES continued. The Bn relieved the 6/York+Lancs in the Rt Sub sector of Rt Section of CARENCY BRACQUEMONT sub sector. Relief complete by 7pm. Relief Letter No. 8 Appx 13 C6 (7/LT SUTTON JR) proceeded to Guignon at 10.30 p.m. No. 8 to remain under the now system of Platoon training & will be in 13	

(A7092). Wt. W12859/M1293. 75,000. 1/17. D. D. & L., Ltd. Forms/C2118/14.

Army Form C. 2118.

WAR DIARY
or
INTELLIGENCE SUMMARY.
(Erase heading not required.)

Instructions regarding War Diaries and Intelligence Summaries are contained in F. S. Regs., Part II. and the Staff Manual respectively. Title pages will be prepared in manuscript.

Place	Date	Hour	Summary of Events and Information	Remarks and references to Appendices
	14th		Demonstration Platoon	
			Major PIPER proceeded to Elebon to take command	
		1/30pm	A Cas T.M. Bombardment was carried out by the 3 Inf. Bde. (1st Aus. la. Opr.) on our left. Retaliation on our sector was nil	No 38
	15th		The enemy shelled EXETER DUMP, FOSSEWAY, + O.B.L communication trench in the morning, night with 10·5 cm. + 15 cm. Hows. Mixing of Gas+ Blue × Cross.	No 1 of June
	16th		2/Lt F. PARKER, M.C. proceeded on Paris leave to ENGLAND Capt. SUFFOLK proceeded on Special Leave to ENGLAND.	
		11.30a.m.	Gas was projected from G.30.6.99.20 (34 Bde. Front) on to HOBART TR. M19.20.55.40 – H26.8.6. Chlorine and unknown green light mass freed. Shortly after zero from enemy trenches opposite our front. Felt no retaliation followed.	No. 40
	17th		The vicinity of EXETER DUMP was again shelled at 4 pm + 9pm 2/Lt BOLTON proceeded on Leave to ENGLAND.	
		12 noon to 1pm	Contact flying was successfully carried out by the Corker + a Contact Aeroplane.	

Army Form C. 2118.

WAR DIARY
or
INTELLIGENCE SUMMARY.
(Erase heading not required.)

Place	Date	Hour	Summary of Events and Information	Remarks and references to Appendices
	Aug 17th		The shelling of EXETER DUMP was reduced between 11 p.m. & 1 a.m. this was with 77 mm.	
	19th		Hostile artillery very quiet. A successful daylight patrol was carried out by —	
			LT. C.A.B. THORBURN 73 Co. 2/LT F.O. BATES A Co.	
			Strength 9 O.R. BORDER NORTH	
			Route Starting 9.50.95.90 to Sap. 9.50.a.9 into GERMAN front line	
			Time of starting 5.30 p.m.	
			Object (1) To examine GERMAN front line. (2) Obtain identification if possible.	
			The patrol succeeded in entering the GERMAN front line & made a thorough examination. Inspected the enemy's trench & found a number of such bomb dumps. They also had an number of Lewis plates in position.	Sketch N°1 N°2 N°3 W.I.7
			One of the enemy were seen down at 9.50.ay a.9. & O.T. coming towards the patrol. Our men Lying in wait for him however his him. Enemy apparently charged direction & could not seen again. The patrol returned at 8.45 p.m.	

WAR DIARY or INTELLIGENCE SUMMARY

Army Form C. 2118.

Place	Date	Hour	Summary of Events and Information	Remarks and references to Appendices
	Sept 20		The Lewis held by "A", "B" & "D" Coys were busied during the early morning with 77 mm + TMs etc. L/Cpl BULLEN + Smith (C+A 7.01) - 2/Lt MAISHMENT proceeded on leave to ENGLAND. Congratulations were sent to the Rugby Football party of the 5th Brigade Square of the signal releaxe & Composed on their leave. (Letter to the 1st Corps Notes the re held 16 of 2/3 Cavl. (Arab t.o.) 1 Squay etc. Batt. Despatching one Coy. H.D. Horse (arrayed) and was delivered 2 more A geo bombardment and capture out by a 5 + 6 hours on Royal opposite the Brigade sector.	
	21.9		The 1st LEICESTERS (47th Inf Brigade) (16th Division) relieved 3 Inf Brigade (1st Devons) on our left. the vicinity of EXETER DUMP + 13 M.17 Q. was attack unnecessary between 9 + 11 pm. were at 77 mm. On the night 21/22nd LITHBURN, 2/Lt 39785 + St. BURGESS remained the same route as on the Davis patrol go. 19th. was the same object in view taking mules then 30.9. of 9 Q. & 2 men of 6.8.17.9 a under Sgt COOK 45. They left our lines at 9.25 pm + returned at am (22nd). They formed one of the several reported on the 19th to be low entrances to a Dugout who they encountered passing a number of	to exam w/o at 2 Congrats etc. leave Parti heard etc.

WAR DIARY
or
INTELLIGENCE SUMMARY.
(Erase heading not required.)

Army Form C. 2118.

Instructions regarding War Diaries and Intelligence Summaries are contained in F. S. Regs., Part II. and the Staff Manual respectively. Title pages will be prepared in manuscript.

Place	Date	Hour	Summary of Events and Information	Remarks and references to Appendices
	July 22nd		Notice Boards which they pulled down brought back. A dynamo engine was heard working but no sign of the enemy was seen on kennel in the kennel system. A moving party about 20 strong was seen near the enemy 2nd line & artillery fire was brought to bear on this party by one of our planes. 2 hostile Balloons were brought down in flames by one of our planes.	The Corps Commander comments:- A good & interesting patrol, useful & is due to all ranks & it is hoped to be repeated on another suitable night
	22nd	6.30am	Two hostile Balloons were brought down in flames by one of our planes.	
			The remains of B.n.H.Q. was shelled between 6 & 7 p.m. 2nd Batt: received orders to do 3 extra days in the Line prior to the Devereux being relieved by the 15th Division. Ewinden (5 N.C.Os) from 13th Royal Scots arrived to reconnoitre the sector.	
	23rd		The shelling of EXETER DUMP was repeated between 5.30 & 7.30pm otherwise quiet.	
	24	7.30am	In connection with an operation by the 2nd Division on our left a sight & smoke screen was placed across our front by the Artillery 11 to 2	

WAR DIARY

or

INTELLIGENCE SUMMARY.

(Erase heading not required.)

Army Form C. 2118.

Instructions regarding War Diaries and Intelligence Summaries are contained in F. S. Regs., Part II. and the Staff Manual respectively. Title pages will be prepared in manuscript.

Place	Date	Hour	Summary of Events and Information	Remarks and references to Appendices
	Aug 24		Retaliation was only slight	
		3pm	A hostile balloon was brought down in flames by one of our planes	
	25th		The Bn. was relieved by the 13th Royal Scots (15th Division) on the left sub-Section during the morning & marched to GRENAY where they entrained on light Railway at 3.30 p.m. & proceeded to CHELERS arriving at 7.30pm. From there they marched to Billets at MAGNICOURT (M.35 d.0.11) arriving at 9 pm	See Appx No. 44
			The Battn. less №6 Coy. PIPER marched from COURCIEUX to MAGNICOURT arriving at 12.30 p.m. after a 4 hrs march. Capt. E. BOURDAS & 36 O.R. rejoined the Battn. from 6th R.E.C. 2/Lt. WALKER proceeded on leave to ENGLAND	
MAGNICOURT	26th		2/Lt. FOSTER proceeded on leave to ENGLAND Companies resting & cleaning up	
	27th		A warning order was received about 6 a.m. for all Reinforcements Hd. Stores to go to the Dump & for the Battn. to be ready to move off at 2 hrs notice. Lorries called for Reinforcement at 9 a.m. Later the moving off notice was extended to 12 hrs	See Appx No. 44

Army Form C. 2118.

WAR DIARY
or
INTELLIGENCE SUMMARY.
(Erase heading not required.)

Instructions regarding War Diaries and Intelligence Summaries are contained in F. S. Regs., Part II. and the Staff Manual respectively. Title pages will be prepared in manuscript.

Place	Date	Hour	Summary of Events and Information	Remarks and references to Appendices
MAGNICOURT	Aug 27 (cont)		An hours demonstration was given by M.G Platoon, under 2/Lt SUTTON who have been in special training, at 10 am to Officers & NCOs of the Batt. The C.O. inspected the fighting strength of Companies 2/3/44 at 2 pm.	
	28th		Companies training 9 am - 12.30 pm, training programme being arranged by Platoon Commanders. Maj. Earl DAVIS (Batt Commander) arrived the training General during morning. Specialists training from 2 - 3 pm. On (crossed out) Lecture was given at MONCHY BRETON at 5.30 pm. Two Officers & 9 O.R.s from each Coy & 1 Officer & 30 O.R.s from B.H.Q. were present being conveyed by lorries to the Lecture hall.	
	29th	1.45 a.m.	Orders received from 33rd Bde Hd qrs Bath to be ready to move at short notice. Lorries report at Bn stores to take surplus baggage to DUMP at TINCQUES, at 9am.	App. 1146.
		1.15 pm	Battalion parades ready to entrain on arrival of lorries.	
		3 pm.	(illegible) Brass Band & entraining commenced	
			Battalion billeted at Ostreux Camp, (illegible)	Offrs (illegible)

P. D. & L., London, E.C. (35001) Wt. W1771/M2031 750,000 5/17 Sch. 52 Forms C2-0/14

WAR DIARY or INTELLIGENCE SUMMARY.

Army Form C. 2118.

Place	Date	Hour	Summary of Events and Information	Remarks and references to Appendices
	29th	4p.m.	Nomes start and arrive at Ablaination. ECURIE (M9 LENS M40/00) at 9.10 p.m. Battalion is billeted on huts for the night.	J.K.
ECURIE	30th	10 a.m.	C.O. proceeds to reconnoitre route for next move & to make arrangements for moving into the line. N.E. of MONCHY LE PREUX.	
		2 p.m.	Batt. marches via ST. LAURENT - BLANGY - ATHIES - to ORANGE HILL 1 mile S.W. of FEUCHY - halts for tea & proceeds at about 8.15 p.m. into the line. Transport and rations located just S.E. of FEUCHY near FEUCHY Chateau. Reaches 21 Oftero 630 Chateau. Strength of Battalion moving into trenches 21 officers 630 O.R. Battn. is disposed in support to 6th Lincs R. & 7th Leics R. who are holding an outpost line N.E. of BOIRY-NOTRE-DAME	J.K.
TRENCHES	31st.		Hostile artillery active carrying out area shoots during day on Bryan Sector.	J.K.

J.K. Ingram Lieut.
J. Ketherwood Deserter
by O.C.

No 27

25ᵃ

J.B Service Eversum the Honoured Judge

Asar Biswas

for

September 1918.

Army Form C. 2118.

WAR DIARY
INTELLIGENCE SUMMARY

September 1918

(Erase heading not required.)

Place	Date	Hour	Summary of Events and Information	Remarks and references to Appendices
NEAR BOIRY NOTRE-DAME	1st		Day quiet. Operations proceed for the attack by Canadian Corps L.H. British Division on DROCOURT-QUÉANT line on 2nd inst. Soon relieved 7th I.R. Regt. on left sector of Battalion front.	240/6
"	2nd		Attack on Drocourt-Quéant line as before commenced at 5 a.m.	
"	3rd		Day quiet. A very good patrol done by Lt. Featon & Sgt. Butler who went from Casualties inflicted on enemy — our casualties — Lt. Clarke wounded.	1 O.R.
"	4th		Day quiet. Usual work done on defences & improving posts. Part of our division relieved through night between MONCHY and BOIRY.	
"	5th		Day quiet. Enemy aeroplane coming to view — one machine gun taken by enemy brought down in flames.	
"	6th		Day quiet. 1 man Lewis & Company.	
"	7th		Rain. Relieved by 9th Yorkshire Regt. Relief completed by 12. 9.45 a.m. Batt: proceed to Watch in train. Enemy M.G. Gun Lewis	
"	8th		Day spent in cleaning up, inspections, baths &c.	
ARRAS	9th		Day spent in cleaning up, inspections, baths &c. the town during the day.	
"	9th		Weather inclined to be rainy. Company Training carried on during week. Inter Works Brey V.R. gone again on leave. 2Lt. S. Wakerley proceeded on leave. Company training carried out as yesterday.	
"	10th		2Lt. J. A. Wylie proceeds on leave. Artillery action — artillery of enemy	
"	11th		Batt: relieves 9th York. Regt., in right subsection of BISCUIT & BOIRY Posts, see app. 50 complete by 1.30 a.m.	

Army Form C. 2118.

WAR DIARY
or
INTELLIGENCE SUMMARY.

(Erase heading not required.)

Instructions regarding War Diaries and Intelligence Summaries are contained in F. S. Regs., Part II. and the Staff Manual respectively. Title pages will be prepared in manuscript.

Place	Date	Hour	Summary of Events and Information	Remarks and references to Appendices
BOIRY-Notre-Dame.	13th Oct.		Heavy artillery active on Batn. area. No casualties. Situation quiet. Work on defences partially be carried out. Enemy aircraft active. 9 Hostile planes during the free day. One enemy plane chased by one of our scouts and crashed in our own lines.	
	16th.		Day quiet on the whole. 6 O. Cap's area shelled at 8 p.m. - 2 men wounded. Night. Other relieves commanding officer who proceeded to garrison duty to pass.	
	17th.		Day quiet. C.O. on leave. C.O. 2/Lt Hampshire Regt. came up as relieves Batn. scout officer.	
	18th.		That quiet. Heavy shelling of our Battery positions in vicinity of BOIRY between 5, 6 p.m. and 10 p.m. 2/Lieut. K.G. Shelton Lieut C.F Kingdom join Batton from leave. the latter take over Adjutant from 2/Lt Ray.	
	19th.		J.O. Proceeded on leave. Captain Eaton relieved him the 2ic by 2/Lt Stephens (capt. 3) Ref. (H.Rifles H.E. Dyn.) and Brevet 6 Croquis in TROHY. Reserve Defences (Eastern) moves to TINCOURT from ST AUBIN.	
FECHY.	20th Oct.	10am	Batn entrained and brigades to over billets at MAGNICOURT-en-COMTE (Mayor's Rd.) Ost. 5. arriving at 2 pm. whole billet reformed by 3 pm. Remy marched from TINCOURT	
MAGNICOURT Bet.		6 pm	Batn. cleaning up talking etc Lieut J Sanders proceed to 1/1 Infy Leather Camp THROTTLES. To take over studies experimental Regt cent. T.O. Kelling batty Hery head welcoming from leave. No till died that have conducted by race.	

WAR DIARY
INTELLIGENCE SUMMARY

Army Form C. 2118.

Instructions regarding War Diaries and Intelligence Summaries are contained in F.S. Regs., Part II. and the Staff Manual respectively. Title pages will be prepared in manuscript.

(Erase heading not required.)

Place	Date	Hour	Summary of Events and Information	Remarks and references to Appendices
MORENCOURT en-Comte	Sept. 24		Companies training in vicinity of billets from 9.0 am - 12.30 pm.	
		2pm	Another practice of move to BERNEVILLE.	
			Batn. carried out an attack scheme under the CO. during afternoon. The scheme to include a move by Motor Buses, and an enemy.	Apps. 52, 53.
	24	4.15am	Orders received as regards the programme.	
		7pm	Those carried out according to programme. Batn. moved by M.T. Buses, and the preparation made for move of Batn. into the line for future Operations.	
	25	4pm	Batn. moved to VIS-en-ARTOIS by lorry, arriving at 8pm, and engaged in carrying out sec. 54.	
			reconnaissance of the area, and relieving trenches from the Batn. 2 miles S. of the village to the S.W. front line trenches.	
VIS-EN-ARTOIS	26	10am	400 succeed to Batn HQ to secure instructions to make reconnaissance of battle positions.	
		7pm	Batn. moved forward & reached in readiness of DROCOURT-QUEANT line just E. of CHERISCOURT, arriving at 9.30pm. Very heavy rain during the night.	
	29		The Canadian Corps to which the 11th Div belonged attacked the German positions E. of the Canal-de-Nord for dawn (say 5.30 am) when a heavy barrage opened.	App. 55
			At 2.40 pm (165 min (0.5 am)) the 1st place of the attack having been successful to Batn. who were the 3rd line when in reserve to the Regy. which in turn were in support to positions on the BUISSY SWITCH S.E. of the 52nd and Bn. W.S. Bn. moved forward to positions on VILLERS - les CHERISCOURT arriving at 10 am.	
			Reports are received during the day that 11th Div. captured their objectives (BOURLON Ridge - OISY-le-VERGER). Little doing in the Batn. area. during the General Attack.	

NIL

Army Form C. 2118.

WAR DIARY
INTELLIGENCE SUMMARY.
(Erase heading not required.)

Instructions regarding War Diaries and Intelligence
Summaries are contained in F.S. Regs., Part II.
and the Staff Manual respectively. Title pages
will be prepared in manuscript.

Place	Date	Hour	Summary of Events and Information	Remarks and references to Appendices
NEAR VILLERS-LEZ CAGNICOURT	27th	6am 6.30pm	2/Lt. 1 Officer per Coy. and Bath. scouts reconnoitre bridges across the CANAL du NORD. Weather — Slight rain at 3am — afterwards dry and bright. For time table of operations see appendix 55.	
	28th		The Batn. remain at BUSSY SWITCH awaiting orders. Batn. Scouts move to CHERISY to position 3 mile N.W. of Battalion. Transport lines are established in CAGNICOURT. R.O. and platoon commanders reconnoitre bridges across CANAL du NORD. The O.C. 2nd Cdn. Regt. leaves BUSSY SWITCH and goes the CANAL du NORD, taking up a position just S. of SEUCHY L'ESTREE. Weather cold and showery.	
	29th	6am 9.30am	A minor enterprise N.E. of EPINOY was attempted by the 22nd Bde. but failed owing to strong machine gun position. Batn. moved about 1000 x in a S.E. direction and took up a position in BUSSY SWITCH vacated by 8th Lincoln Regt. the previous evening. The Colonels of which the Batn. is composed left the 61st Army today. Companies carrying, mining and general duty an attack scheme. The L.O.C.sends his most cordial congratulations to the 11th Bde. on the success of the attack. Weather cold and showery.	
	30th		Batn. remain in same position as yesterday and continues training. Weather — cooler, cloudy with showers at intervals.	

A.B.Matthews Lt. Col.

www.ingramcontent.com/pod-product-compliance
Lightning Source LLC
Chambersburg PA
CBHW081243170426
43191CB00034B/2028